Classic Overtures
for Timpani

from Mozart to Wagner

compiled by ...ldenberg

Table of Contents

CORIOLAN

Overture

TIMPANI in C.G.

L. van Beethoven, Op. 62

EGMONT

Overture

TIMPANI in **F, C**

L. van Beethoven, Op. 84

TIMPANI in **F, C**

5

Overture No. 3
to the Opera LEONORE (Fidelio)

TIMPANI in C G

Ludwig van Beethoven, Op. 72a

PROMETHEUS

Overture

TIMPANI

L. van Beethoven, Op. 43.

ROMAN CARNIVAL
Overture

Timpani in **A E**

Hector Berlioz, Op. 9

Timpani in A E

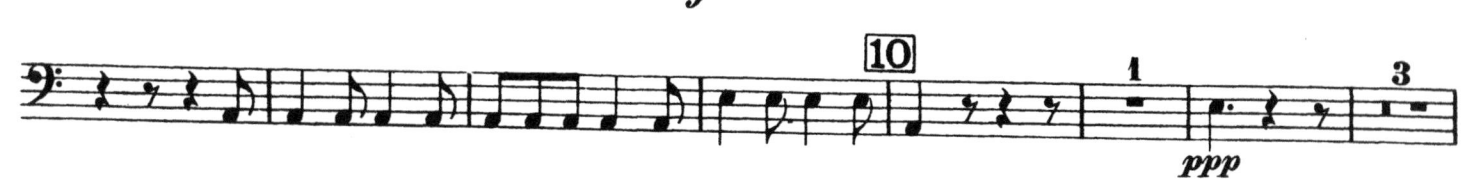

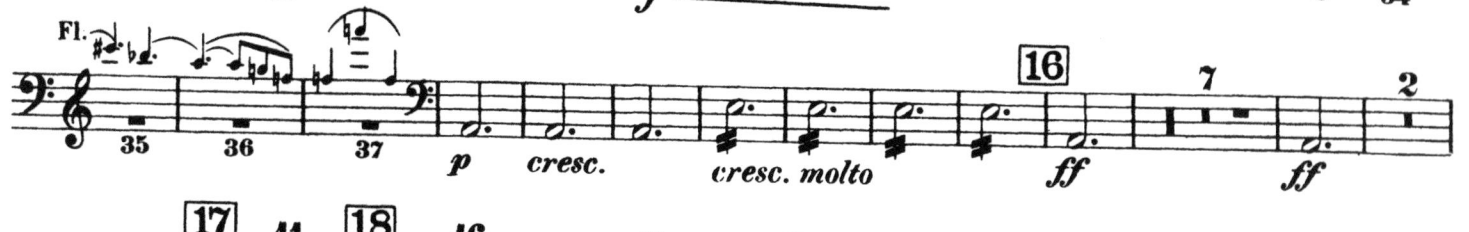

Academic Festival Overture

TIMPANI in G · C · D.

Johannes Brahms, Op. 80

TIMPANI.

Carneval.
Ouvertüre.

Timpani.

Ant. Dvorák, Op. 92

Timpani.

Les Préludes.

TYMPANI

F. Liszt.

OVERTURE
THE HEBRIDES
(Fingal's Cave)

Felix Mendelssohn Bartholdy, op. 26

TIMPANI in B, F♯

Allegro moderato.

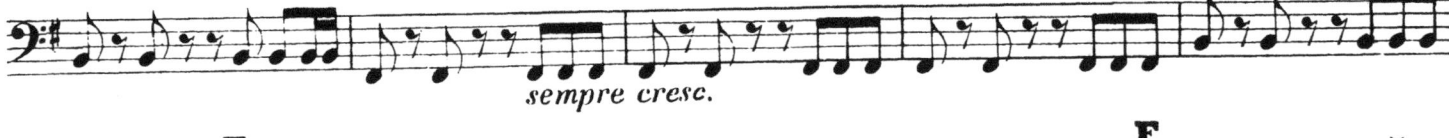

MIDSUMMER NIGHT'S DREAM

Overture
op. 21
TIMPANI in E.

Felix Mendelssohn Bartholdy

Allegro di molto.

OUVERTÜRE

zu Ruy Blas

von

FELIX MENDELSSOHN-BARTHOLDY

OP.95.

TIMPANI in C. G.

TIMPANI.

Ouverture zur Oper „Così fan tutte".

Timpani in C. G.

W. A. Mozart, K. V. 588.

OVERTURE
to the opera
DON GIOVANNI

TIMPANI in D.A.

Wolfgang Amadeus Mozart, K. 527

The Magic Flute
Overture

Tympani

W. A. MOZART

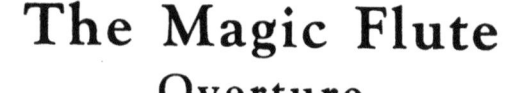

Le Nozze di Figaro (The Marriage of Figaro)

Overture

Timpani in D-A

Wolfgang Amadeus Mozart, K. 492

Il Seraglio
Overture

Timpani
(C-G)

TIMPANI in C.G.

W. A. Mozart, K. 384.

Ouverture
zur Oper „Wilhelm Tell".

Pauken in **E, H.**

G. Rossini.

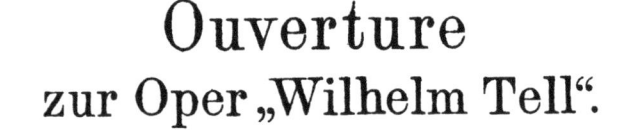

Ouvertüre
zur Oper „Die diebische Elster".

Pauken in **E. H.**

G. Rossini.
Bearb. von G. Kogel.

The Barber of Seville

Overture

Timpani
E–B

Pauken in E. H.

G. Rossini.

Andante maestoso.

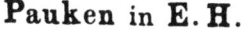

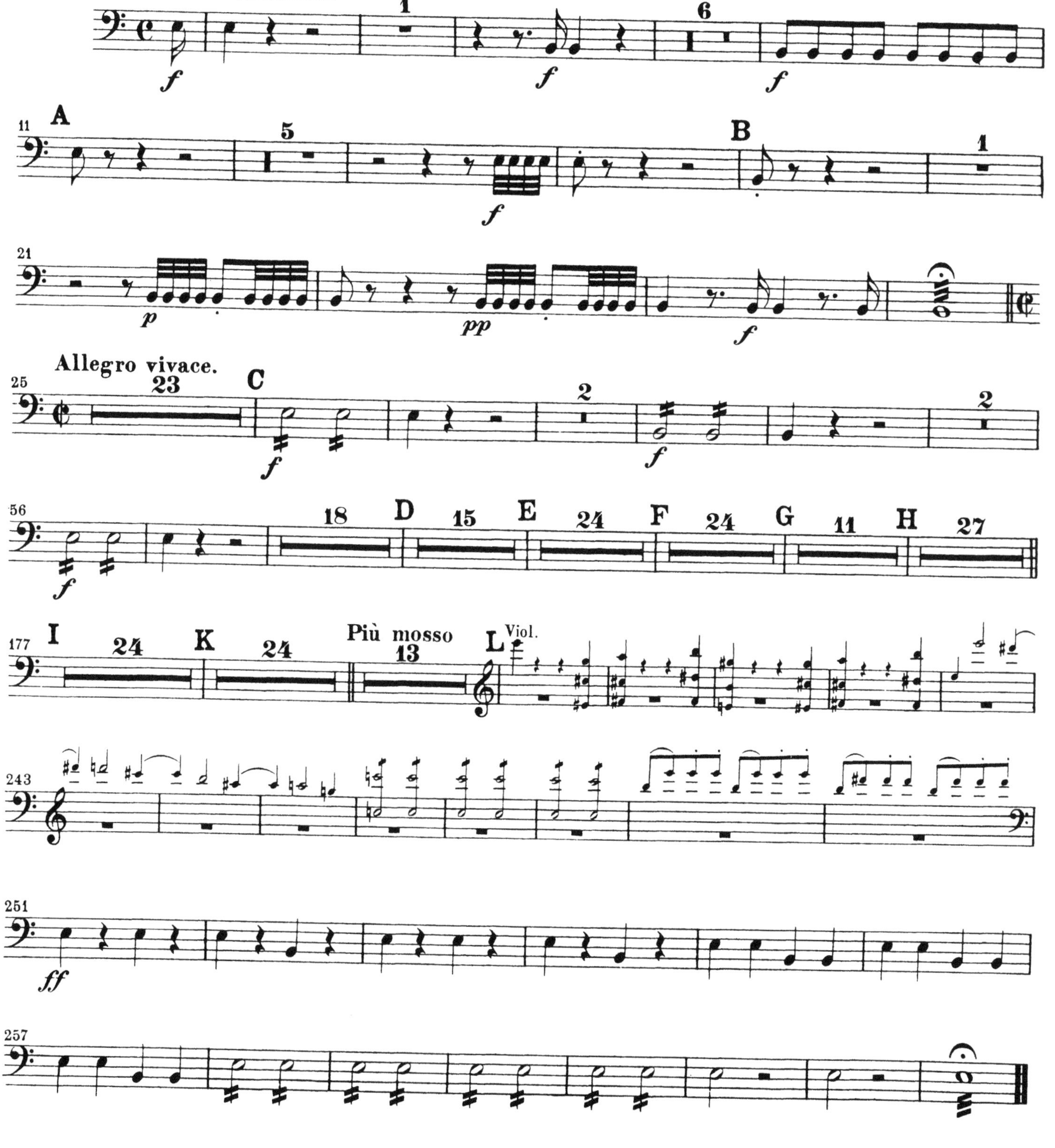

Ouverture zur Zauberharfe.

Pauken in C.G.

Franz Schubert.

Pauken in C.G.

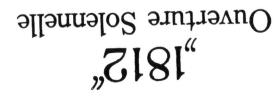

Schlagzeug

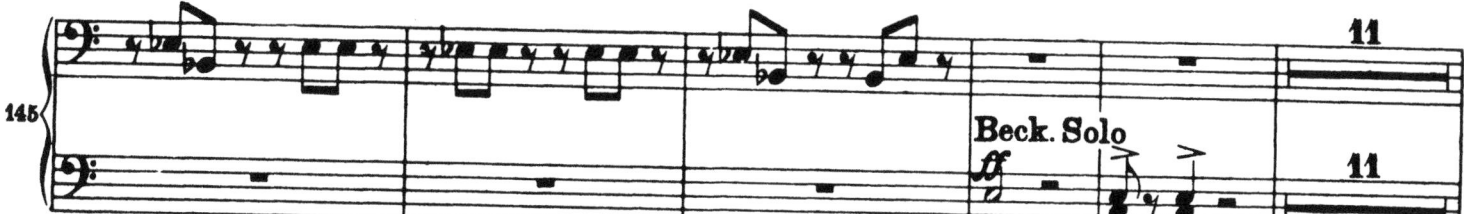

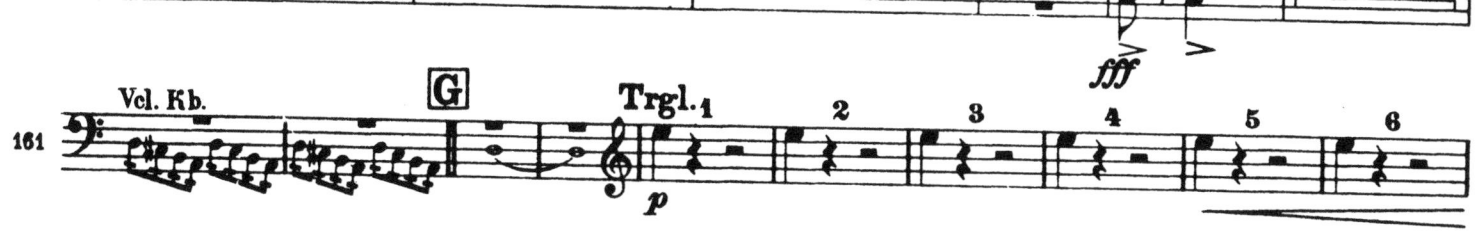

Schlagzeug

Schlagzeug

Romeo et Juliette.
Ouverture-Fantaisie.

Timpani.

P. Tschaïkowsky.

Timpani.

OUVERTURE

zur Oper:

„Der fliegende Holländer."

Le Vaisseau fantôme.—*Il Vascello fantasma*.

in D u. A. (Ré & La.)

Pauken. (Timpani.)

Richard Wagner.

Allegro con brio.

Pauken.

RICHARD WAGNER.

VORSPIEL
zu der Oper
DIE MEISTERSINGER ZU NÜRNBERG.

PRELUDE
to the Opera
THE MASTERSINGERS OF NUREMBERG.

TIMPANI in C & G.

must be always played.

With small orchestras, the notes representing the absent instruments (indicated by * in the parts)

Ouvertüre
zur Oper „Euryanthe".

TYMPANI

C. M. von Weber.

Ouvertüre
zur Oper „Oberon".

Pauken in D.A.

CARL MARIA VON WEBER

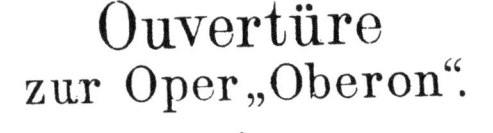

About the Author

MORRIS GOLDENBERG is the author of two other books for the percussion student and performer, *"Modern School for Xylophone . . ."* and *"Modern School For Snare Drum . . ."*. He is a staff percussionist at NBC television studios in New York at present. In addition to his many recording and performing activities, the author is also a faculty member of the Juilliard School of Music, the Manhattan School of Music and the National Orchestral Association.

Mr. Goldenberg has long felt the need for a collection containing standard orchestral literature which would supplement the basic timpani methods already available. In choosing the overtures for this volume, he has been guided by the inherent musical role the timpani part plays in each composition.